Running a Race

How you walk, run and jump

Steve Parker

FRANKLIN WATTS

New York • London • Toronto • Sydney

© 1991 Franklin Watts

Franklin Watts, Inc.
387 Park Avenue South
New York, NY 10016

Library of Congress Cataloging-in-Publication Data
Parker, Steve.
    Running a race / Steve Parker.
       p.   cm. — (Body in action)
    Summary: Describes what happens to the human body while running a
race and provides tips for technique in such areas as warming up,
breathing, and recovering from the race.
    ISBN 0-531-14096-2
    1. Running for children—Juvenile literature.   2. Running for
children—Physiological aspects—Juvenile literature.   3. Running
races—Juvenile literature.   [1. Running.   2. Running races.]
I. Title.   II. Series.
GV1061. 18.C45P37   1991
796.42—dc20   90-31110
                                                      CIP AC

Printed in Great Britain

Medical consultant:
Dr. Puran Ganeri, MBBS, MRCP, MRCGP, DCH

Series editor: Anita Ganeri
Design: K and Co.
Illustrations: Hayward Art
Photography: Chris Fairclough
Typesetting: Lineage Ltd, Watford

The publisher would like to thank Andeep Patel for appearing in the
photographs of this book.

CONTENTS

The body in motion

You are always moving. Even when you are asleep, and there is no movement on the outside of your body, there are various parts inside you that are still moving. Your heart beats, your lungs breathe in and out, and your intestines push food through your body. When you run a race at full speed, your whole body moves, from your eyebrows to your toes. These movements are made by muscles, bones and joints. They are controlled by nerves running from your brain.

△ Your body needs regular exercise to keep your muscles, bones and joints fit and healthy. Sport is one of the best ways of getting exercise.

▷ The human body can do an amazing range of movements. It can bend over, twist around, and push itself up on its arms. These movements are good warm-up exercises before a race. They flex your joints and get your muscles working. How many can you do?

push-up

leg stretch   **trunk-twist**

STRENGTH FACTS

• The human body is capable of some amazing feats of strength. But this takes skill and practice. If you try a new sport without learning the correct movements, you may badly damage your bones, muscles and joints.

• A weightlifter uses small weights at first, and practices lifting them using the right technique.

• After a while, the muscles used for lifting become larger and powerful, and the bones and joints become stronger.

• Some weightlifters can lift over 990 pounds above their heads. That's more than the weight of 15 ten-year-old children!

step-up

squat-jump   **toe-touch**

The body's framework

Your body has a framework inside it, like a scaffold of strong girders. The framework is your skeleton, and it is made up of dozens of bones. Bones are strong, tough and quite stiff. They keep your body from flopping into a jellylike heap on the floor. Some bones help to protect the soft parts of your body from knocks and injuries. For example, the skull in your head protects your brain. Your ribs protect your heart and lungs inside your chest.

△ The long, strong bones in your arms and hands allow you to grip the tracksuit zipper and pull it down. You are now ready for the start of the race.

BONE FACTS

stirrup bone

• An adult person's body has about 206 bones in it.
• A newborn baby has more than 300 bones. Some of these join together, or fuse, as the baby grows up.
• Your largest bones are in your thighs. They make up about a quarter of your total height.
• The smallest bones are only the size of match heads. There are six, three deep inside each ear. They are called the hammer, anvil and stirrup.
• Healthy bones are hard and tough, but not rigid or brittle, like the dry bones in museums. They can bend slightly so they do not snap.

THE SKELETON

skull (cranium)

Each of the bones in your skeleton has two names. One is the everyday name, the other is a scientific name, used by doctors, biologists and other experts. Here are some examples of everyday names, with scientific names in brackets.

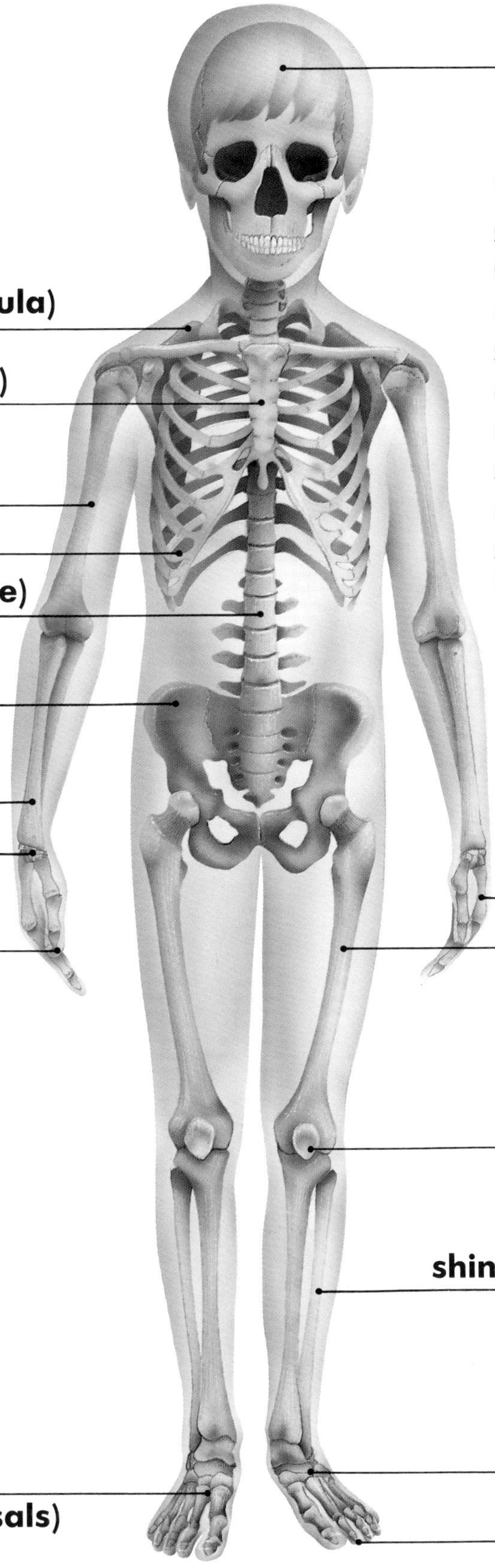

shoulder blade (scapula)

breastbone (sternum)

upper arm bone (humerus)

ribs (ribs)

backbones (vertebrae)

hipbones (pelvis)

forearm bones (radius and ulna)

wrist bones (carpals)

finger bones (phalanges)

palm bones (metacarpals)

thighbone (femur)

kneecap (patella)

shin bones (fibula and tibia)

anklebones (tarsals)

foot bones (metatarsals)

toe bones (phalanges)

7

Your flexible body

Your bones are strong and quite stiff, so how is your body so flexible? Many bones are not attached to each other. They come together at flexible joints. In a joint, the end of each bone is covered with a smooth, shiny substance called cartilage. The cartilage lets the bones rotate against each other easily, without rubbing. Across a joint, the bones are held together by strong straps called ligaments. These keep the bones from coming apart and control their movement.

△ As you crouch down at the start of the race, many of your joints bend. The main ones are in your ankles, knees, hips and back.

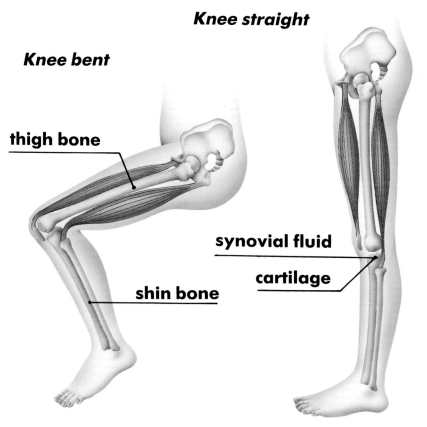

Knee straight

Knee bent

thigh bone

synovial fluid

cartilage

shin bone

▷ Your thigh and calf bones almost touch inside your knee. They are kept apart by a very thin layer of fluid, called synovial fluid. This works like oil in a car engine. It makes the parts slippery, so they do not rub.

8

HOW FAR CAN YOU BEND?

Your knee joint is like a hinge. It bends your leg forward and backward, but not sideways. Your elbow is similar. Hold your arm out, palm up, and move your elbow. Compare its range of movements with those of your shoulder. The shoulder is a ball-and-socket joint. It is one of your most flexible joints.

JOINT FACTS

• The knees are the biggest single joints in your whole body.
• The ankle has seven main joints and dozens of ligaments. It has to be very strong, to carry the weight of your body when you run.
• The smallest joints are between the tiny bones inside your ear.
• Some bones are stuck together at joints and cannot move. The 22 bones in your face and skull form one rigid part. You can see these bones below. The wiggly lines where they are fused, or joined, are called sutures.

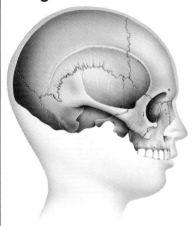

joints (sutures)
braincase (cranium)
cheek bone (zygomatic bone)
upper jaw (maxilla)

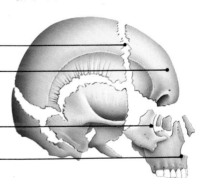

Pulling power

Bones form the framework for your body, and joints allow the bones to move. But muscles provide the power to move your whole body. A typical muscle has a bulge in the middle, and two long, tapering ends, called tendons. Each tendon is firmly fixed to a bone. A muscle works by becoming shorter, or contracting. As it shortens, it pulls the bones, and so bends that body part. Most movements are carried out by several muscles working as a team.

△ Some of the muscles in each leg pull hard to straighten your joints. Your feet push back against the ground, and thrust your body forward for a flying start to the race.

▷ As you run, the muscles in your hips and buttocks move your upper leg. They are attached to your hipbone at the top, and to your thighbone at the bottom. Your thigh muscles bend your knee, and your calf muscles bend your ankle.

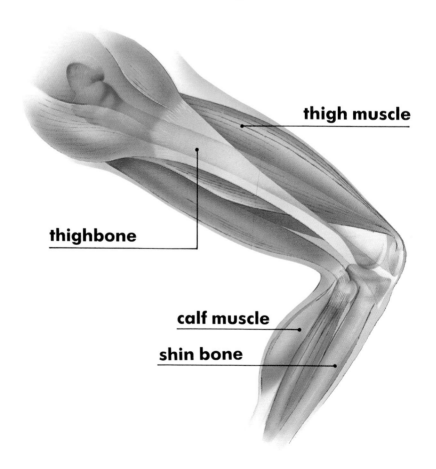

thigh muscle

thighbone

calf muscle

shin bone

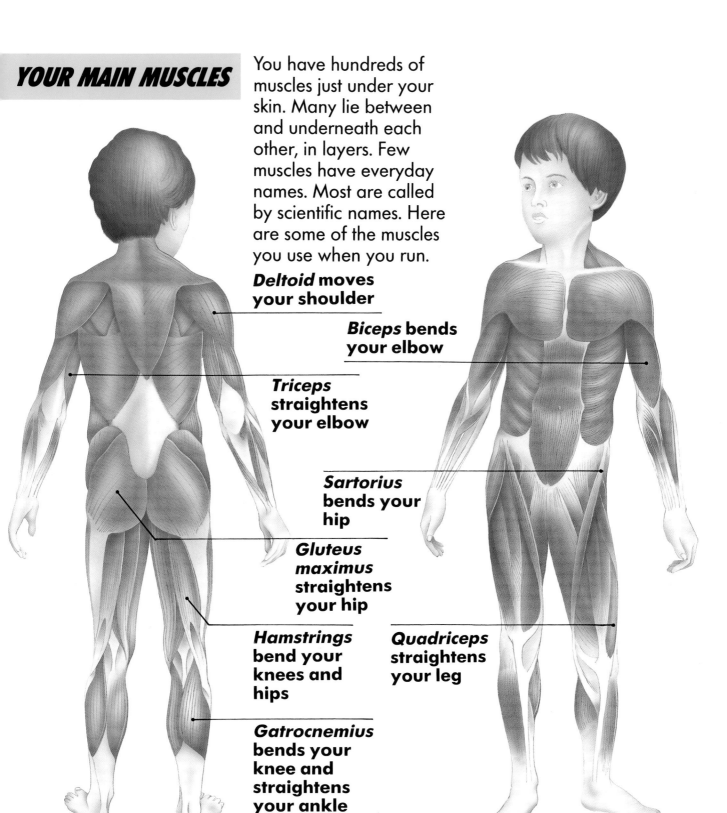

YOUR MAIN MUSCLES

You have hundreds of muscles just under your skin. Many lie between and underneath each other, in layers. Few muscles have everyday names. Most are called by scientific names. Here are some of the muscles you use when you run.

Deltoid moves your shoulder

Biceps bends your elbow

Triceps straightens your elbow

Sartorius bends your hip

Gluteus maximus straightens your hip

Hamstrings bend your knees and hips

Quadriceps straightens your leg

Gatrocnemius bends your knee and straightens your ankle

11

Inside a muscle

▽ Below you can see an enlarged view of each part of a muscle. There are about a dozen muscle fibers in each bundle. The longest fibers are up to 12 inches long.

A muscle is covered by a thick skin called the epimysium. Inside, a muscle is made up of bundles of tiny threadlike fibers. A big muscle, such as one in your leg, has hundreds of fibers. The fibers themselves are made up of even smaller threads, called myofibrils. A muscle pulls by shortening its myofibrils to almost half their usual length.

epimysium **bundles of muscle fibers** **bundles of myofibrils**

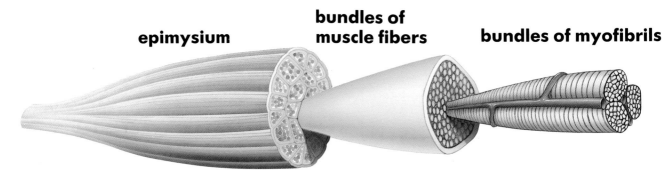

MUSCLE FACTS

• You have more than 600 muscles in your body which help to move your bones.
• These muscles make up about two-fifths of your body weight.
• The biggest muscles are the quadriceps and gluteus muscles in your thighs and in your buttocks.
• The smallest muscles are in your ear. They pull on your tiny ear bones when sounds are too loud. This stops the delicate hearing parts of your inner ear from being damaged.

gluteus muscles

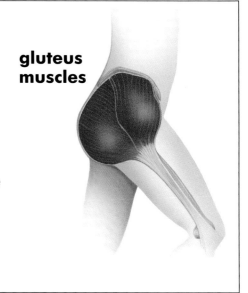

MUSCLE CONTROL

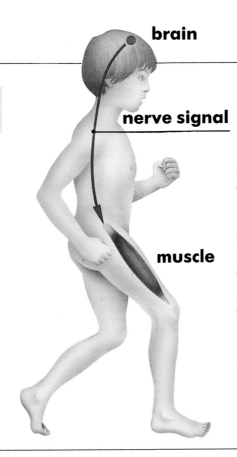

brain

nerve signal

muscle

Most muscles do not work on their own. They need messages to tell them when to get shorter. These messages are tiny electrical signals, brought by nerves from the brain. When you want to move, a signal flashes from your brain, along a nerve to the proper muscle. Here it spreads through the muscle and makes it shorten. With practice, you do not have to instruct each muscle separately. Your brain can control whole teams of muscles almost automatically. This is why you hardly have to think about common movements like walking and running.

HOW DOES A MUSCLE WORK?

Make an arm from two cardboard tubes with paper fasteners at the "elbow." Make a hand out of cardboard. Use a piece of string as the muscle. Attach it near the wrist and pull it 2 inches shorter. How far does the hand move? Now attach the string near the elbow and pull it 2 inches. How far does the hand move? Where a muscle is attached affects how far it moves a bone.

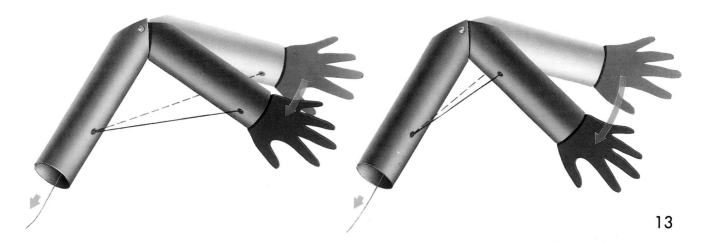

13

Muscle partners

Muscles can only pull. They cannot push. So they usually have partners which pull in opposite directions. One of the partners shortens to pull the body part one way, and the other partner shortens to pull it back again. As one muscle pulls, the other muscle relaxes so it can be stretched more.

△ As you run, one set of muscles pulls to swing your arm forward.

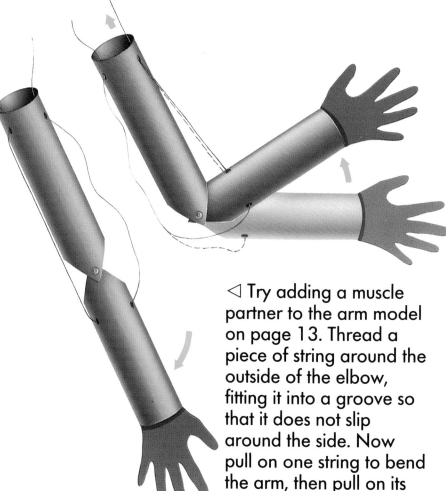

△ Then their partners work to pull your arm back again.

◁ Try adding a muscle partner to the arm model on page 13. Thread a piece of string around the outside of the elbow, fitting it into a groove so that it does not slip around the side. Now pull on one string to bend the arm, then pull on its partner to straighten it.

MUSCLES WHICH DON'T PULL ON BONES

Some muscles do not pull on bones. They pull on other muscles, or even on themselves. Among them are some of the 30 or so muscles in your face. These help you make faces, from a broad grin to a grumpy frown. Your eyelids and lips contain straplike muscles which become straighter as they get shorter and close your eyes or mouth. Muscles in your cheeks pull up the sides of your mouth to make you smile. There are also many muscles without bones inside you. Some of these are shown below.

MUSCLES INSIDE YOU

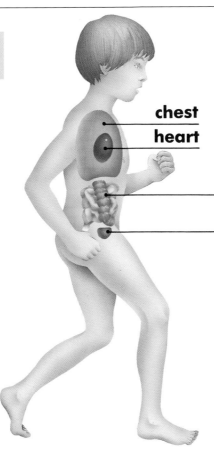

chest

heart

intestines

bladder

The muscles in your chest work every few seconds, to make you breathe. They carry on even while you are asleep.

Your intestines are like tubes with rings of muscles in their walls. These muscles shorten to squeeze and push food along inside the tubes, as the food is mashed up and digested.

Your heart is like a muscular bag, full of blood. As its muscle fibers shorten, the bag gets smaller and squeezes the blood out (see page 18).

The muscles in your bladder stretch as the bladder fills with urine. After a while they cannot stretch any more. When you go to the bathroom, they shorten to push out the urine.

Puffing and panting

A muscle, like a car, needs fuel. In fact, a muscle uses two kinds of fuel. It uses nutrients from food which contain energy (see page 20). It also uses oxygen from the air you breathe. The oxygen passes across the thin lining of your lungs to the blood on the other side. Your blood carries the oxygen around the body to your muscles. Muscles make you exhale stale air and then inhale fresh air with each breath.

△ As you run, your muscles work harder and harder so they need more and more oxygen. This is why you breathe faster and deeper, to get more air into your lungs.

▷ When you breathe in, your rib muscles pull your lungs up and out. Your diaphragm muscles pull your lungs down, making them bigger. As you breathe out, your rib muscles relax and let your ribs fall back. Your diaphragm relaxes and lets your lungs spring up and get smaller.

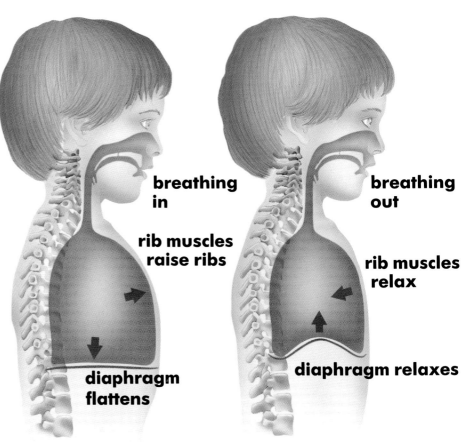

breathing in

rib muscles raise ribs

diaphragm flattens

breathing out

rib muscles relax

diaphragm relaxes

BREATHING FACTS

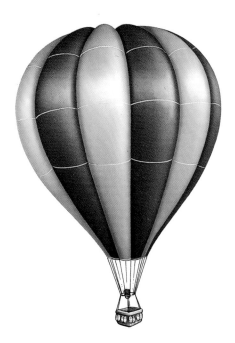

- At rest, a pair of lungs holds about 3¼ quarts of air.
- A very deep breath doubles this to 6½ quarts.
- An average person at rest breathes in and out about 15-20 times each minute.
- After a hard race, you breathe about 15 times more air in and out than you do when resting.
- During the night you breathe about 4-5 cubic yards of air in and out. You would need to sleep for six months to fill up a hot-air balloon.
- Each lung has more than 300 million tiny air bubbles. They give it a huge surface for taking in oxygen.
- Flattened out, these bubbles would cover about 96 square yards — the size of half a tennis court.

HOW BIG ARE YOUR BREATHS?

Fill a kitchen measuring cup with water and turn it upside down in a deep bowlful of water, so it stays full. Support its rim on small cups. Breathing normally, bubble your out-breaths through a straw into the cup. After about five breaths, mark the cup at the surface of the water inside it. When you empty the cup and turn it right side up, read the volume at the mark. Divide this figure by the number of breaths, to find how big each of your breaths is.

Pumping blood

△ At the winning tape, your heart is pumping hard and fast, to supply extra fuel and oxygen to your hard-working muscles.

Your blood takes in oxygen from your lungs, then it flows back to your heart. The heart is a two-sided pump powered by muscles. Blood from the lungs flows into the left pump. It is squeezed out and flows around your body's blood system, supplying oxygen, nutrients and fuel. It then flows back to the heart's right pump. From here it flows to the lungs again, for more oxygen, before going back to the heart's left pump.

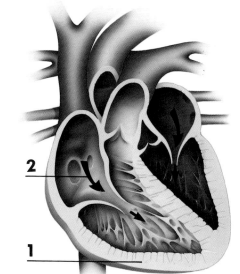 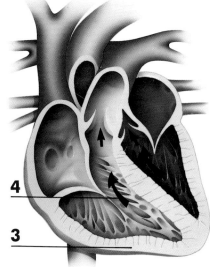

▷ Your heart squeezes about once every second, to make the blood flow around your body. Each pump of your heart is called a heartbeat.

1 Heart muscle relaxes, so heart swells with incoming blood.
2 Blood enters heart from the lungs and the rest of the body.

3 Heart muscle contracts.
4 Blood is squeezed out to the lungs and the rest of the body.

HOW FAST DOES YOUR HEART BEAT?

You can test how fast your heart beats by taking your pulse. Each time your heart beats, it sends blood surging along the blood vessels. The blood presses against the elastic walls of the vessels, making them bulge slightly. You can feel this bulge in the blood vessel in your

wrist. Place one or two fingers in the hollow of your wrist below your thumb, and feel for the pulsing vessel just under your skin. (Don't use your thumb, because it has a small pulse of its own, which could be confusing.) Count how many surges there are in one minute. This is your pulse rate.

HEART FACTS

• There are 6½ quarts of blood in a human body, continuously flowing around in a nonstop circuit.
• At rest, an average adult's pulse rate is 75 beats each minute (see page 23).
• One heartbeat pumps about 2 fluid ounces of blood from each side of the heart.
• This means that at rest, a heart pumps enough blood to fill a bathtub in about 13 minutes.

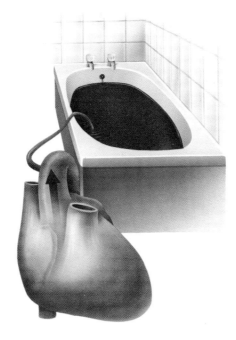

• During a hard race, your pulse rate speeds up to more than 150 beats a minute. The amount of blood pumped in one beat rises to as much as 6½ fluid ounces.
• So, during a race, the heart would pump enough blood to fill a bathtub in just over two minutes!
• An adult's heart weighs about 8 ounces about as much as two medium-sized apples.

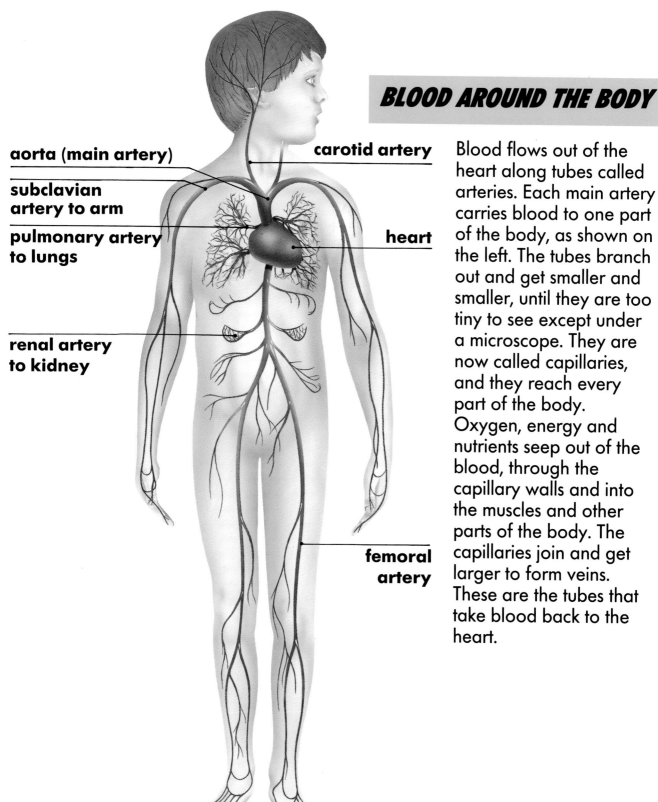

aorta (main artery)

subclavian artery to arm

pulmonary artery to lungs

renal artery to kidney

carotid artery

heart

femoral artery

BLOOD AROUND THE BODY

Blood flows out of the heart along tubes called arteries. Each main artery carries blood to one part of the body, as shown on the left. The tubes branch out and get smaller and smaller, until they are too tiny to see except under a microscope. They are now called capillaries, and they reach every part of the body. Oxygen, energy and nutrients seep out of the blood, through the capillary walls and into the muscles and other parts of the body. The capillaries join and get larger to form veins. These are the tubes that take blood back to the heart.

Aching muscles

△ Ease the pain of cramp by gently but firmly stretching the cramped muscle.

You get a cramp when a muscle suddenly goes out of control and gets shorter. This is called a muscle spasm. You feel a sharp pain as the muscle becomes hard and knotted. A cramp can affect any of your muscles, but it often happens when you suddenly start using a muscle which you do not normally put to hardwork. It may also happen if the blood vessels to the muscle cannot supply enough blood to provide the oxygen and energy it needs.

KEEP YOUR MUSCLES FROM ACHING

Immediately after a race, your heart and lungs work very hard to provide your muscles with enough oxygen and energy. After doing any type of exercise, you should always do a few "cooling-down" exercises. This will help your heart and lungs get back to normal gradually, and your muscles and joints from suddenly becoming stiff. Try doing some of the exercises below.

arm swings

leg shakes

gentle jogging

Cooling down

Hard-working muscles make a lot of heat. But your body cannot work properly if it gets too warm. So it has several ways of cooling itself down. The blood vessels in your skin get wider so they can carry more blood, and this blood lets heat escape from your body. It also makes you look flushed. You also have sweat glands that pour watery sweat onto your skin. As this dries, it draws heat from the body.

△ Panting after a hard race replaces the oxygen which your large leg muscles have used up when you were running.

hair flattened

hair raised

sweat pore open

heat lost

sweat pore closed

▷ When you get too hot, your sweat glands produce lots of watery sweat, which flows up curly tubes on to the surface of your skin.

hot skin

cold skin

22

GETTING BACK TO NORMAL

After a race, your heart still beats fast. It slowly goes back to normal. To measure how long this takes, first take your pulse (see page 19).

Then do some hard exercise like running fast. Take your pulse again right afterward. Keep taking it over the next 5-10 minutes, and draw a graph of the results. In general, the faster your pulse returns to normal, the fitter you are.

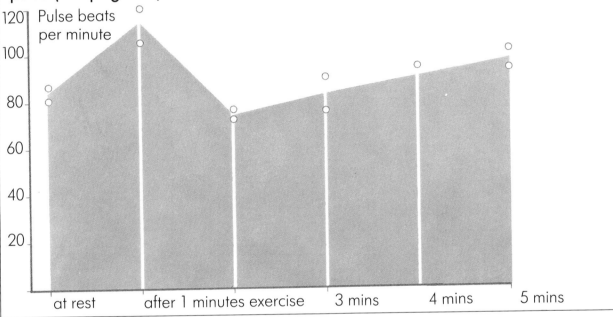

Pulse beats per minute

120
100
80
60
40
20

at rest | after 1 minutes exercise | 3 mins | 4 mins | 5 mins

PULSE FACTS

• Sleeping babies have a pulse rate of about 120 each minute.

• As you grow, your pulse rate slows down. By the age of 10 years, it is below 100.

• Adult pulse rates are about 70 for men, and nearer 80 for women.

• Very fit people, such as top-class athletes, have pulse rates as low as 50. This is because their hearts are large and very strong.

• Exercise makes your heart beat faster. So does being nervous or worried, as you may feel before taking a test or examination.

• Astronauts, at the time their rocket blasts off, and racing drivers have very fast pulse rates. Their pulse rates may be 200 or more!

23

Refueling

△ A drink of juice or a special high-energy sports drink gets energy to your blood, and so to your muscles, quickly after the race.

Fuel enters your body as food. In your digestive system, nutrients from the food pass into your blood system and are carried to all parts of your body (see page 20). These nutrients contain energy. Your muscles convert the energy into movement. Busy muscles need more fuel than lazy ones. If you are very active, you need to eat more food.

jet airliner   ⅕ mile (984 feet)

car   6 miles

person running   93 miles

▷ This chart shows how far your body and various machines could travel on the energy found in 40 2-ounce bars of chocolate. These bars contain about as much energy as 1 quart of gasoline.

person cycling   310 miles

HOW MUCH ENERGY IS THERE IN FOOD?

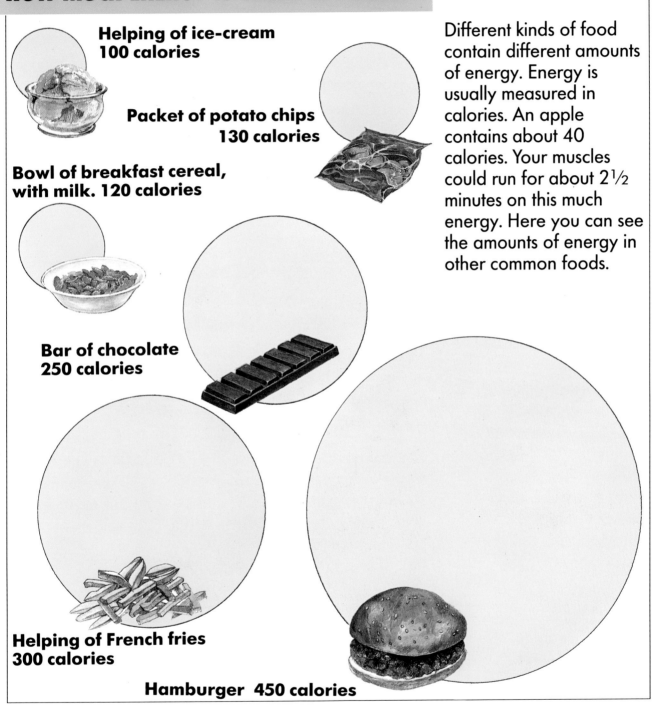

**Helping of ice-cream
100 calories**

**Packet of potato chips
130 calories**

**Bowl of breakfast cereal,
with milk. 120 calories**

**Bar of chocolate
250 calories**

**Helping of French fries
300 calories**

Hamburger 450 calories

Different kinds of food contain different amounts of energy. Energy is usually measured in calories. An apple contains about 40 calories. Your muscles could run for about 2½ minutes on this much energy. Here you can see the amounts of energy in other common foods.

Staying strong and supple

Exercise helps keep your joints flexible and supple. Otherwise they might become stiff and painful. Exercise also helps keep your bones and muscles strong, so they do not become soft and waste away. These muscles include the ones that move your skeleton, help you breathe and make your heart work. Exercise also helps increase your stamina, so your muscles can work for longer without getting tired. To stay fit and healthy, remember the "3 Ss" – suppleness, strength and stamina.

△ When you take part in an active sport, such as soccer, badminton or swimming, you use many different muscles and joints. This helps keep your body in good condition.

HOW STRONG ARE YOUR SHOULDERS?

You can test the stamina of your shoulder muscles. Hold your arms out straight and level in front of you, with your palms facing down, for as long as you can. The muscles in your shoulders will soon begin to ache and tremble. Finally you have to stop. Time how long this takes. Now practice the exercise three times a day, for one week. Then, time yourself again. See how much the stamina in your shoulder muscles has improved.

WHICH SPORTS ARE GOOD FOR YOU?

This chart shows how various sports improve your suppleness, strength and stamina. The more stars a sport has, the better it is for you.

SPORT	Suppleness	Strength	Stamina
Badminton	★★★	★★	★★
BMX biking	★★★	★★	★★
Cycling	★★	★★★	★★★★
Gymnastics	★★★★	★★★	★★
Hockey	★★★	★★★	★★★
Jogging	★★	★★	★★★★
Rowing	★★	★★★★	★★★★
Soccer	★★★	★★★	★★★
Squash	★★★	★★★	★★★★
Swimming	★★★★	★★★★	★★★★
Tennis	★★★	★★	★★
Weightlifting	★★	★★★	★★
Windsurfing	★	★★★★	★
Yoga	★★★★	★	★

SPORTS FACTS

• The human body is not the fastest-running or the longest-jumping in the animal world, but it has good all-around abilities.

• The world's fastest sprinters run 100 meters (110 yards) in less than 10 seconds. They reach a top speed of over 22 miles an hour. They train their bodies for power and speed.

• Long-jumpers can leap almost 9 meters (10 yards), more than the width of a singles tennis court.

• High-jumpers clear a bar about 8 feet above the ground.

• The marathon race is some 26 miles long. Top runners complete it in just over 2 hours, at an average speed of 12 miles an hour.

• Machines help the human body to go farther, faster. On land, racing cyclists reach 43 miles per hour over a short sprint. That's twice as fast as a runner.

• In the water, the fastest swimmers go at about 5 miles per hour. But a top-class rower can scull at almost 12.5 miles per hour.

Things to do

To see how flexible you are, gently bend various joints of your body. You can compare them with gadgets around your home, which use the same types of joints. Try these to start with:

Keeping your elbow and wrist straight, swing your arm at the shoulder. You should be able to move it up, down, around, and even backwards. Your shoulder is a very flexible ball-and-socket joint (see page 9). It is like the joint in a computer joystick.

Balance on one leg. Bend your other leg at the hip, and hold its thigh steady. Gently try to bend your knee so that it moves from side to side. No? Your knee is a strong hinge joint, that only moves to and fro. It is like the hinge joint in an anglepoise desk lamp.

HANDY JOINTS

Look at the back of your hand, with your fingers spread. Move the bottom knuckle of your first (index) finger, where it joins your palm. It can wiggle up and down, and from side to side. Now do the same with the next knuckle up. This one only moves up and down, but it can bend almost double. The next knuckle bends even less. The many special joints in your hand work to give you a strong or delicate grip.

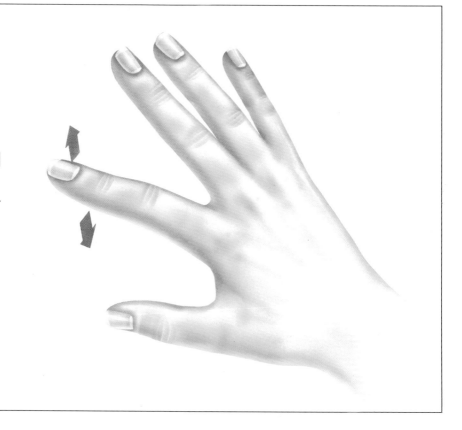

28

HOW FAST DO YOU BREATHE?

To find out how fast you breathe, make a breathing rate chart like the pulse rate chart on page 23. Follow the instructions given there, but count your breaths instead of your pulse. ("One breath" is a breath in and out again.) Normal breathing rate at rest is about 15-20 breaths a minute. When do you breathe fastest? Is it immediately at the end of the race, or a minute or two later?

SPORTS DIETS

Find out about special meals eaten by athletes. Weight-lifters need lots of meat and fish for protein to build up their muscles. Long-distance runners need plenty of sugary and starchy foods for energy.

HIGH-FUEL FOODS

Look on food packet labels for the energy contents of different foods. They are usually given both in calories Using the information on page 25, work out how far you could run on a serving of various foods. For example, compare a slice of pizza with a sausage, or a drink of fruit juice.

BUNCHES OF MUSCLES

Move parts of your body and feel for the tensed, bunched-up muscles which are doing the pulling. Sometimes the muscles are not where you would expect them to be. For example, hold out your arm and hand, palm up. Wiggle your fingers. Notice the muscles moving in your forearm, and the long tendons in your wrist which carry the muscles' pulling power to your finger bones.

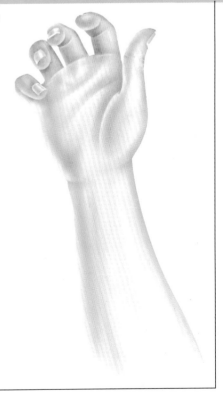

Glossary

Blood   A red liquid that flows round and round the body inside tubes, called blood vessels. It carries nutrients and energy-giving materials from digested foods. These "leak" through the walls of the blood vessels, to all body parts.

Bone   A single part of your skeleton. Bones are made of the protein collagen and various minerals, including calcium and phosphorus.

Breathing   Muscle-powered movements of the chest that make the lungs bigger and smaller. This sucks in fresh, oxygen-rich air and then blows out stale air.

Cartilage   The smooth, shiny substance that covers the end of a bone inside a joint. Cartilage lets the bones slide past each other easily, without rubbing or wearing.

Diaphragm   A sheet of muscle under the lungs, at the bottom of the chest. As it shortens and flattens, it makes the lungs bigger, for breathing in air.

Energy   The "power" to make things happen, ranging from a chemical process inside the body to the whole body running along at top speed. Life depends on a regular supply of energy, which is contained in food.

Epimysium   The thick, tough "skin" that covers a muscle. Holes in it allow nerves and blood vessels to pass into the muscle.

Heartbeat   One complete pumping cycle of the heart. This sucks blood into the heart and then squeezes it out again, around the lungs and body.

Joint   Where two bones come together. Some joints are fixed and rigid, as in the skull. Other joints are flexible, where both bones can move.

Ligaments   Strong elastic-like straps around a joint, that hold the bones together. The ligaments stop the bones moving too far and coming apart completely.

Resources

Muscle A body part specialized for becoming shorter (contracting). As it does so, it pulls on the bone, muscle, or other body parts to which it is fixed.

Myofibril A microscopic thread inside a muscle. Many myofibrils bunched together make a muscle fiber, and many muscle fibers bunched together make a whole muscle.

Nerve signal A tiny electrical message that travels along a nerve. Nerve signals from the brain are carried along nerves to the muscles, to tell them when to shorten.

Nutrient A "building block" substance that the body uses for growth, or for repairs.

Tendon The tapering, rope-like end of a muscle, which anchors it to a bone or other body part.

Skeleton The strong framework inside your body, made of about 206 bones.

United States Government Printing Office
Superintendent of Documents
Washington, D.C. 20402

(Request leaflets on health and fitness.)

BOOKS TO READ

The Mind-Body Problem by Rebecca Goldstein.
New York; Dell, 1985.

Keeping Fit Handbook for Physical Conditioning and Better Health by Fred Neff.
Minneapolis; Lerner Publications, 1977.

Exercise and Fitness by Brian Ward.
New York; Franklin Watts, 1988.

Running Skills by S. Peach.
Tulsa; EDC Publishing, 1988.

The Human Body and How it Works by Angela Royston.
New York; Warwick, 1991.

Index